THE
PRINCIPAL
APPROACH
WORKBOOK

DR. DAVID SUTTON

To order additional copies you can contact us at our website:
www.drdavidsuttonministriesinternational.org
email us at david@drdavidsutton.com
or
Write to us:
Dr. David Sutton
P.O. Box 3917
Sarasota, Florida 34230

Table of Contents

WELCOME TO YOUR NEW LIFE

The Principle Approach to the Steps

WELCOME TO YOUR NEW LIFE

Introduction

I F YOU HAVE THIS BOOK in your hand you have likely read "The Principle Approach" or have a copy. If not I would recommend you avail yourself to this book. This workbook can be used as a supplement to your reading, a follow up or even can be used as a stand alone exercise.

Each section will address a specific principle, followed by relevant questions to better help you absorb and process the material. This should not be considered an exhaustive study on the recovery from addictions, but more a training tool to advance those who have the desire to embrace recovery and a whole life.

I have started with a questionnaire designed to assist you in identifying if you are in fact addicted to alcohol or drugs. You can substitute the words alcohol or drugs for anything that you are struggling with. For example, gambling, pornography, food, and cigarettes whatever you are unable to put down on your own.

I am calling this the "Addiction Test". Take the test and see how you measure up. This test has been put together to be a guide for self-evaluation only. It should not be considered a clinical diagnosis.

Respond to the following questions with *yes* or *no*. Answer as honestly and truthfully as possible.

The Addiction Test:

1. *Does my drinking ever make my family members unhappy?* **Yes No**

2. *Has drinking or using drugs negatively affected my reputation?* **Yes No**

3. *Have I ever lied to cover my drug use or drinking? Have I lied to my family, friends or even to myself?* **Yes No**

4. *Have I ever driven with others in the car while under the influence of alcohol or drugs?* **Yes No**

5. *Do I ever feel guilty about drinking and using?* **Yes No**

6. *Has anyone ever asked me to stop drinking or using drugs?* **Yes No**

7. *Do I crave a drink or a pill at a regular time daily?* **Yes No**

8. *Do I have trouble waking up or getting out of bed in the morning after I drink or use?* **Yes No**

9. *Do I want to have a drink the next morning to settle down?* **Yes No**

10. *Has spending money on alcohol or drugs kept me from buying necessities, such as food or clothing, or from paying the rent or mortgage?* **Yes No**

11. *Do I drink to cover up feelings of inadequacy or lack of confidence?* **Yes No**

12. *Do I use drugs or alcohol as a method of escaping from life or problems?* **Yes No**

13. *Have I ever been in trouble with the police or court because of my drinking or drug use?* **Yes No**

14. *Do I suspect that my use of alcohol or drugs has increased over the past few months?* **Yes No**

15. *Have I ever tried to quit or cut back my drinking or drug use, just to find myself back where I started?* **Yes No**

16. *Has my efficiency at work or home decreased since drinking?* **Yes No**

17. *Have I ever been treated by a doctor for addiction, or problems related to drinking or using?* **Yes No**

18. *Do I use drugs or drink alone, or need to keep my use a secret?* **Yes No**

19. *Have I ever lost a job or work opportunity due to drug and alcohol use?* **Yes No**

20. *Have I ever had a blackout and not been able to remember certain events or periods of time as a result of drug use or drinking?* **Yes No**

21. *Have I ever been in a hospital or institution for my alcohol consumption and drug addiction?* **Yes No**

22. *Do I lower my standards regarding friends and or my environment when partying, using or drinking?* **Yes No**

23. *Is drinking putting my job or business at risk?* **Yes No**

24. *Have I given up a relationship so I could continue drinking and using drugs?* **Yes No**

25. *Have I ever missed time from work because of drinking or using?* **Yes No**

26. *Does my drinking make me careless about others safety or feelings?* **Yes No**

27. *Have I ever thought about suicide since I have been drinking or using?* **Yes No**

28. *Have I ever used alcohol or drugs to help get through a bad situation or even to get through a day?* **Yes No**

29. *Am I ever sick the next morning after I drink or use?* **Yes No**

30. *Am I afraid others will find out about my drinking and drug use?* **Yes No**

31. *Does drinking cause me to have difficulty sleeping?* **Yes No**

32. *Have ever I lied to physician to gain prescription drugs or unnecessary pain medications?* **Yes No**

33. *Do I use alcohol or drugs to feel good, self-confident, overcome shyness, or to forget my problems?* **Yes No**

34. *Have I ever borrowed or stolen money to buy alcohol or drugs?* **Yes No**

35. *Do I have financial problems because of my drinking?* **Yes No**

36. *Do I ever feel remorse after drinking or about my behaviors?* **Yes No**

37. *Have I ever driven a vehicle while under the influence of alcohol or drugs?* **Yes No**

38. *Have I lost time from work due to my using?* **Yes No**

39. *Have I ever quit for a period and found myself drinking or using more as soon as I started up again?* **Yes No**

40. *Do I drink because I am uncomfortable around people?* **Yes No**

So how did you do? What was your score?

Questions answered yes: _____

Questions answered no: _____

If you answered *yes* to any *one* of the above questions, there is a good chance that you have addictive tendencies.

If you answered *yes* to any *two* questions, addiction to alcohol or drugs is likely.

If you answered *yes* to any *three or more* questions, you are definitely an addict, alcoholic and should seek help.

WELCOME TO YOUR NEW LIFE

Step # 1 Admitted we were powerless over alcohol - that our lives had become unmanageable.

PRINCIPLE: *HONESTY*

WELCOME TO YOUR NEW LIFE

Committed people!

S O THINK ABOUT IT. IN order to become an alcoholic or addict you needed to make a commitment to the cause. Some sacrifices needed to be made. Because you took your medications early a couple times doesn't qualify you for membership in the junkie club. You really needed to put a better effort in than that. Just a glass of wine at dinner was not enough. You had to do some serious drinking and mess things up to make it to the big league. Sacrifice everything - - yes that is what it takes; and millions have done just that. Those who are addicted, give up everything for one thing. Recovery suggests, give up one thing and gain everything else.

In order to move out of the cycle of addiction you will need to make an equal and opposite commitment. This is especially true in the area of honesty. The principle of honesty is one that is so indispensable, that in order to ever turn your life around, you will need to get completely honest! Being honest means I won't cheat, lie or steal. It means that I am a person who is trustworthy, sincere and genuine. It means I can be counted on.

Most of those who are addicted cannot truthfully say any of these things. Addicts are powerless over their addiction to alcohol or drugs (other things as well.) Most have a substantial denial system designed to protect their addiction and addictive behavior. They are deliberately dishonest to avoid consequences, cunningly dishonest to have their own way and creatively dishonest to cover their mistakes and bad choices. Anything it takes to protect their addiction and not to have the truth be found out.

To break the cycle of addiction we must get honest. In order to ever get honest, we must find the courage to tell the truth about what we did and who we really are. Truth is hard to come by on our own strength. In order to find truth we must access truth from an external source and assimilate it into what we believe. Once we get truth on the inside, the dishonesty will stop. You have likely heard the verse "And you will know the truth and the truth will set you free." One person added, "but first it will make you miserable."

Honesty extended.

You must admit you are powerless over your addiction, and as the result of this out of control behavior, your life has become unmanageable. If your not sure if this fits, ask a family member if they think it is true. Another option is to simply go back to the addictions test at the beginning of this book and check your score.

In the day that I see the flag of the overwhelming need to prove and establish that I am right, I can be sure I am on the wrong track. We have been deceived by our addiction and our own thinking. Deception that is believed as truth, will have the same effect as if it were true.

When you come to an end of deceiving yourself and have that moment of clarity, it is time to make a change. In the recovery world they call that hitting bottom. You can truthfully say, I have hit bottom. Hitting bottom is where your situation is deteriorating faster than you can lower your standards. Most caught in addiction have lowered their standards to accommodate their addiction. At this point the need to mask everything is necessary. Every bottom has a trap door. Stay there long enough and you will need to find relief. You may choose to pick up your addiction again. This is a place that we need relief. Whatever it takes to make us feel better is the choice. Then ignoring the consequences, we go back into the very destructive behavior that has caused the problems to begin with.

So look at the following questions and answer them as accurately and honestly as you can. **This is an exercise in getting honest.**

1. Describe a situation or problem that ever got better (or worse) by getting high or drunk?

_____

_____

_____

2. Do I see my routine desire to drink or use, as a clear indicator that I am an alcoholic or an addict? How often do you want to drink or use drugs?

_____

_____

_____

3. Who have you lied to about your wanting to drink and why was it you had to lie?

_____

_____

_____

4. List your 3 biggest current life challenges and note any of the problems you have today that come from your addiction.

_____

_____

_____

David Sutton

5.   Is there any situation that will improve through drinking or using? Describe.

_____

_____

_____

6.   Do you see your current situation unmanageable or is it more like unbearable. Has this feeling become normal for you?

_____

_____

_____

7.   What have I given up for my addiction?

_____

_____

_____

All change demands rigorous honesty. The fact that I can identify dishonesty in myself is honesty in progress. At least I am honest about that.

Self disclosure is clearly seeing who you are and what it is that you routinely do. Today you need to be more truthful than you were yesterday. When you become open, things level out and life begins to flow. Telling the truth is the foundation to all recovery.

Honesty comes from within. You cannot be honest operating out of a belief system void of self appraisal and evaluation. Each of the following words represents a behavior that shows a lack of honesty. Which of these traits can you identify in yourself?

Deceit	Yes	No
Distrust	Yes	No
Disrespect	Yes	No
Duplicity	Yes	No
Infidelity	Yes	No
Fraud	Yes	No
Disinformation	Yes	No

Select 2 of the words listed previously and describe how they apply to you.

1. _____

_____

_____

_____

_____

_____

_____

2. _____

_____

_____

_____

_____

_____

_____

David Sutton

THIS IS THE PLACE WHERE you have to break through the walls of denial and say there is something wrong, and it's not about what the substance did to you. You need to flip the coin over and see what it did for you and what it can do for you again. Denial also correlates to the level of pain you are experiencing. You can stay away from an addiction for a period of time, but if you don't actually do something to rehabilitate your life you will end up right back where you started sooner or later. Remember that when the pain in your recovery becomes greater than the pain that will result from the consequences of a relapse—relapse is inevitable.

_____

_____

_____

_____

_____

_____

_____

_____

_____

_____

_____

_____

_____

_____

_____

_____

_____

_____

David Sutton

Step # 2 Came to believe that a Power greater than ourselves, could restore us to sanity.

PRINCIPLE: *HOPE*

WELCOME TO YOUR NEW LIFE

Hopeful people!

O NE OF THE FIRST THINGS that I connected with in my early days of getting sober was derived from this process of accessing hope. The saying that I often heard was:

We came - we came to - we came to believe.

The idea that I came to believe, is in essence an awareness of what could be. The crux of this statement activated for me the process of identification with others who had found sobriety. This spark was the thing that activated very first glimmers of hope in me. Hope that had for so long been deferred. Hope that had seemed like wishful thinking, at best. Lack of hope, was in part, what had been wrong with me from the start, and there was no way to get help without it. Hope, which would become the very substance of the faith that I would later find.

Often the hardest part of believing is not having a foundation of basic hope. It is not the believing, in and of itself, that often is the obstacle; but the preconceived ideas of both hope and belief. A lack of hope is often fostered from past negative experiences from good intentioned people, who were just trying to help. Offering advice and encouragement without any real opportunity. I have heard it expressed, hope without opportunity is just being mean.

Those new to recovery come plagued with layers of fear, anger, shame, and confusion. Feelings of failure, inadequacy, despair and other challenges that they don't even know that they have. When there comes a demand that they believe exactly the way someone says, and do so right now, it is nearly impossible to begin believing. This approach to getting someone to believe, speaks little of mercy, love or forgiveness. Typically it will cause a greater wall to be placed between the one seeking help, and the God who can help them.

Sometimes, the question that produces the greatest effect is not, "Do you believe in Jesus?", or even "Do you believe in God?", but perhaps this should be asked, "Do you believe that I believe?" This very elementary starting point may seem foolish for some; however allowing people to come to their own revelation of God, will open the door later on, to truly introduce them to God, in a life changing way. Just simply to believe in something, may need to suffice to start with.

A Power greater than yourself, typically will leave an element of confusion, for the onlooker. It however is really quite simple. For the person that is trying to find God, obviously the first thing they need to know is where to look. Telling someone to look within, when they have never accepted the

Spirit of God into their life, is paramount to telling them to rely upon their own spirit. This is precisely the thing that they have been doing their whole life. Pull yourself up by your own bootstraps, don't trust anyone, rely upon yourself, etc. This is not an awareness of God, but a consciousness of self. It stands to reason, that this will not succeed; for the very nature of the addictive person is that they are, self centered, self seeking, and operate in a mode of "self-will run riot."

Remember, that if there is to be a power greater than self, then "self" cannot be what is being sought. The person coming into recovery has already exhausted their best plan. Their best plan and their very best thinking got them into the mess that they're in, and they should be told this right up front! Some would speculate that God is within; he is not unless you've taken a measure to ask him in, or that you perceive yourself as God.

When I have a legal problem, I find an attorney; when I am sick and not able to recover, I seek the aid of a doctor; when the car won't run, I find a mechanic, etc. In essence these people become a power greater than me. They are trained and experienced to assist me through the process of overcoming these areas of life's difficulties. There is formed a place of agreement between them and I, that produces power to accomplish that which would be insurmountable by myself. This will work for those that are believers in God and those that are non-believers as well.

The seeker of God needs only look as far as the man standing next to him to find God, providing that the man next to him, knows God. Simply stated, "If you can't find God, guess who's lost?" These first glimmers of God manifesting himself, is through the people of the program, and is often even through those that don't really know him. It's God working through people; that is the essence of all of Christ's teachings.

Remember were dealing with renewing someone's hope. Finding the foundation of hope may serve as a genuine challenge. But, when it is discovered by a tentative young seeker, in their quest to find God, that someone cares about them and loves them unconditionally; hope will return quite rapidly.

The insane behaviors that came as a result of addictive actions are evident. However the problem that truly exists is the absence of hope. The feeling of aloneness, isolation and uniqueness that preceded and accompanied the addiction is where the true challenge is rooted. These perceptions produce the feelings of being "always on the outside looking in," never a part of the crowd and rarely in sync with anyone or anything. This has been described as "terminal uniqueness." Most addictive types perceive themselves with a "loner image." This stereotype image is in their mind normal, and a sure method of drawing attention and sympathy for their blighted life.

Once it is discovered that the things that are being experienced, the behaviors that are being lived out, and the thoughts that are being thought, are common in other people with addiction, the sense of belonging and being normal starts to come back. This renewed hope is the beginning of the journey back normality

I Peter 1:13 says "...be sober, and hope to the end for the grace that is to be brought unto you at the revelation of Jesus Christ; When God is revealed to a man, through man, hope is established."

David Sutton

I Peter 3:15 "…and be ready always to give an answer to every man that asks you a reason of the hope that is in you with meekness and fear:"

Look at the following questions and answer them as accurately and honestly as you can. This is an exercise in identifying areas of your life that lack hope.

1. When are you more comfortable alone or when surrounded by people?

    _____

2. Do you see your continual desire to isolate as normal? _____Yes _____No

3. Do you ever feel as though there is no purpose in your life? _____Yes _____No

    Why? _____

4. Do any of the problems you have today come from a lack of relationships or friendships?
    _____Yes _____No

    Explain: _____

5. Is there any situation that could immediately be improved by connecting with another person?
    _____Yes _____No

    Who? _____

6. Could the unmanageability in your life, what we looked at in the section on honesty, be reduced by allowing others to help you? _____Yes _____No

    In which part of your life would this apply? _____

7. Have you ever found that having spent time with others brought an unexpected favorable result?
    _____Yes _____No

    How? _____

8. Am I willing to try saying yes to invitations that put me in social settings? _____Yes _____No

    If not, why? _____

9. Will I create the relationships in non crisis times to have people to call when I need help? _____Yes _____No

    Who? _____

All change is preceded by self evaluation. The fact that I can identify the need for hope within myself produces hope. At least I am breaking the negative self talk that has me trapped.

So what is it that we need to change to access hope? Breaking isolation and finding solitude.

To get healthy I have to learn the difference between isolation and solitude.

Isolation is entered into by fear, solitude is activated by prayer.

It is normal to want relationships and even to need relationships. We cannot find hope when operating out of a life style of isolation. In the following comparison the words isolation and solitude are given. Isolation represents a lack of hope. Solitude is a place where hope can be developed.

Identify in each comparison which of these traits you can most see in yourself.

1. A. ISOLATION IS A PLACE OF SELF INDULGENCE (HURTING PEOPLE)

    B. SOLITUDE IS SELF DENIAL (GIVING SOMETHING BACK)

    ISOLATION_____ SOLITUDE _____

    EXAMPLE_____

2. A. ISOLATION IS A PLACE OF SILENCE

    B. SOLITUDE IS A PLACE OF COMMUNICATION

    ISOLATION _____ SOLITUDE _____

    EXAMPLE_____

3. A. ISOLATION IS A PLACE OF RUNNING FROM

    B. SOLITUDE IS A PLACE OF RUNNING TO

    ISOLATION_____ SOLITUDE _____

    EXAMPLE_____

4. A. ISOLATION IS DRAINING

    B. SOLITUDE IS A PLACE OF FILLING

    ISOLATION_____ SOLITUDE _____

David Sutton

EXAMPLE_____

5.   A. ISOLATION IS A PLACE OF TURMOIL

      B. SOLITUDE IS A PLACE OF PEACE

      ISOLATION_____ SOLITUDE _____

      EXAMPLE_____

6.   A. ISOLATION IS SELF WILL

      B. SOLITUDE IS SELF CONTROL

      ISOLATION_____ SOLITUDE _____

      EXAMPLE_____

7.   A. ISOLATION IS INCONSISTENCE

      B. SOLITUDE IS A PLACE OF CONSISTENCE

      ISOLATION_____ SOLITUDE _____

      EXAMPLE_____

8.   A. ISOLATION IS A PLACE OF THE FLESH

      B. SOLITUDE IS A PLACE WHERE SPIRIT IS IN CHARGE

      ISOLATION_____ SOLITUDE _____

      EXAMPLE_____

9.   A. ISOLATION IS A PLACE OF WORRY

      B. SOLITUDE IS A PLACE OF WAITING

      ISOLATION_____ SOLITUDE _____

      EXAMPLE_____

10. A. ISOLATION IS A PLACE OF EVIL

B. SOLITUDE IS A PLACE OF LOVE

ISOLATION_____ SOLITUDE _____

EXAMPLE_____

11. A. ISOLATION IS A PLACE OF CONFUSION

B. SOLITUDE IS A PLACE OF WONDER

ISOLATION_____ SOLITUDE _____

EXAMPLE_____

12. A. ISOLATION IS A PLACE OF FEAR

B. SOLITUDE IS A PLACE OF PRAYER

ISOLATION_____ SOLITUDE _____

EXAMPLE_____

13. A. ISOLATION IS A PLACE OF WEAKNESS

B. SOLITUDE IS A PLACE OF POWER

ISOLATION_____ SOLITUDE _____

EXAMPLE_____

14. A. ISOLATION IS A PLACE OF THE DEVIL

B. SOLITUDE IS A PLACE OF GOD

ISOLATION_____ SOLITUDE _____

EXAMPLE_____

David Sutton

LIVED IN A LIFE OF loneliness and isolation. While I am still a very private kind of person and I enjoy my time alone, today it is not isolation but solitude. I found out that there is a huge difference between isolation and solitude. Isolation is a dark cavern of desperation and solitude is a doorway to spiritual growth.

_____

_____

_____

_____

_____

_____

_____

_____

_____

_____

_____

_____

_____

_____

_____

_____

_____

_____

_____

_____

David Sutton

Step # 3 Made a decision to turn our will and lives over to the care of God, as we understood him.

PRINCIPLE: *FAITH*

WELCOME TO YOUR NEW LIFE

People of Faith!

THE FOOL DOES IN THE end what the wise man does in the beginning.

Praying to get sober is wise. Our influence on the future is what we do now here in the present and the most effective thing we can do is to pray. Correspondingly faith without works is dead, the more we act in the present, the greater our faith will become.

In spiritual growth, you will always be more convinced by what you have discovered than by what others have found. Go from being dependent on others to being dependent on God. He is the source of our direction. Too many people base what they believe, do and say on what others believe and say. God is best known by revelation not explanation.

God uses ministers, leaders, books, TV and others to speak into our lives. But it is not enough that what they say is right. Faith will only work when we believe it for ourselves and place a demand on it. The most important convictions of our lives cannot be reached on the word of another.

John Wesley said, "When I was young I was sure of everything; in a few years, having been mistaken a thousand times, I was not half so sure of most things as I was before; at present, I am hardly sure of anything but what God has revealed to me personally."

Go from knowing what others believe to knowing what you believe.

The substance of hope that we discussed in the last lesson is, at least in its change to, formative stages, is a very natural thing. It is derived from the realm sight. Remember we walk by faith, not by sight.

The higher level of walking in the spiritual realm is a faith walk; however this should never be confused with the need to understand how to walk in the natural dimension of sight. Walking by sight is a prerequisite to entering into a comprehension of faith.

Walking by sight involves the lower levels of responsibility toward ones family. A job paying bills, spiritual understanding and in many cases personal health and hygiene. This also includes being able to see the need for clearing up past legal matters, indebtedness, and moral failure. In essence, it is regaining the focus to begin again to live life.

We will take this process to a higher level than just human or natural hope; it elevates this hope into the sphere of faith. The thing that moves us from hope forward to operating in the faith level is what is called "the evidence of things not seen." This is, in all practicality, the beginning of the belief system that God does and will intervene in the affairs of man. There are many who have believed in God, seen God work through others, have prayed to God, have seen answers to prayer, but still doubt that God is interested in the plan and outcome of their personal life.

To find recovery, acknowledgment of God must go beyond just believing that He is. Seeing that God "is," and seeing that God "does," are two different concepts. Acknowledging that God is personal enough to have an interest in me, my life and my family is often far removed from simply saying, yes there is a God.

Most people, even in the church society, believe that God can do anything, but are often reluctant to distinguish the belief that He will. The lack of differentiating the differences that exist between their own limited beliefs and what is truth, is a common trap that keeps people from finding God's best for their lives.

One would have to only read a small portion of scripture to see that God will move on your behalf, if you simply ask. Yet many go on in fear of the future, being overwhelmed with concerns over finances, accepting sickness as God's plan for them and experiencing broken relationships on all sides.

For those who have a relationship with God this seems to be perhaps too elementary to consider. But for those who are desperate and dying of addictive behavior, it is paramount. They, for the most part, don't understand God, life, or you for that matter. They are looking through a "dark glass" and life is real fuzzy. The thing that they do know is fear, pain, anger, and distrust. For them life has become a series of disconnected episodes that have brought immense confusion, strife, disappointment and failure.

Many have come and received salvation, just to later return back to their addiction. The reason was not that their experience with God wasn't genuine; it was simply not carried far enough to provide the transformation they needed. Once they relapsed back to their addiction, the very foundation of their belief system was undermined. So we are actually talking about making a decision to surrender our life into God's care. This can be a scary and sometimes difficult proposition.

CS Lewis said, "The terrible thing, the almost impossible thing, is to hand over your whole self—all your wishes and precautions—to Christ. But it is far easier than what we are all trying to do instead. For what we are trying to do is to remain what we call ourselves."

I cannot surrender and remain in control at the same time. I have to believe God can do for me what I can't, and what's more He will.

To come to the belief that God is willing to do for you what you cannot do for yourself, requires a real life demonstration. To find "the evidence of things not seen" requires a face to face encounter with someone who has that evidence in their life.

The verse says *"...without faith it is impossible to please Him: for he that comes to God must believe that He (God) is, and that He is a rewarder of them that diligently seek Him."*

Once the intervention of God in their life has begun faith will materialize. Those who are without God are looking for real evidence of Him. Because without this transforming God power, there is no possibility of life change.

Faith can be increased at any time simply by increasing the "substance of our hope" and the "evidence of the unseen world." The truth is that we can, by virtue of increasing the elements of faith, increase our faith.

"We made a decision. It was not made for us by the drugs, our families, a judge or probation officer, therapist or doctor. We made it. For the first time since that first high, we have made a decision for ourselves." (The Basic Text)

Making a Decision is based on the following:

1. *The corresponding information connected to the choice.*

2. *Compromises in your life and the things that are non-negotiable.*

3. *Personal life experience in making choices.*

4. *Other people's influences.*

5. *Active belief systems we are currently operating by.*

6. *Expectations of the outcome of our decisions.*

7. *Willingness to live with the outcomes once we choose.*

Look at the following questions and answer them as accurately and honestly as you can. This is an exercise in identifying your ability to make choices.

1. *When you make decisions do you evaluate the information that is available or do you go by how you feel?* _____Yes _____No

   Example: _____

2. *Do you normally ask for the input of those around you before making life decisions?* _____Yes _____No

   Example:_____

3. *Do you have individuals that you can go to for accountability
    in your choices? _____Yes _____No*

    If yes, who? _____

    If no, consider who you could connect with? _____

    *Do any of the problems I have today come from a lack of good
    decision making process? _____Yes _____No*

    Example:_____

4. *Is there any choice in my life today that could immediately be made by connecting with another
    person?
    _____Yes _____No*

    Who? _____

    Example: _____

5. *Could the unmanageability in your life that we looked at in the section on honesty
    be altered by making a different series of decisions? _____Yes _____No*

    Name one decision that this applies. _____

6. *Have you ever found that having spent time with others brought an unexpected favorable
    result?
    _____Yes _____No*

    Who? _____

    Example: _____

7. *Can you identify wrong expectations that have caused you to choose a wrong pathway?
    _____Yes _____No*

    Example: _____

8. *Will considering the reasonable outcomes of your choosing cause you to make better choices?
    _____Yes _____No*

    Give an example of how this would apply: _____

David Sutton

Your ability to trust God or believe God for your needs and wants is proportionate to your knowledge of God.

We cannot build anything on "God as we don't understand Him." Useless debates about the unknowability of God, cannot lead to your will being empowered to make good choices. The point is, do you believe God loves you? Do you believe God works through people? Can get to the understanding that God is not mad at you?

Here are some of the Characteristics of God

1. **Communication**: He is speaking more than I am listening.
    When I listen He is always saying something.

2. **Justice**: There is an old saying that God looks out for drunks, puppies
    and babies. Justice will be presented for everyone.

3. **Mercy**: The steadfast love of the Lord never ceases, "They are new every morning;
    great and abundant is your stability and faithfulness." (Lamentations 3:23 AMP)

4. **Mystery**: He hides revelation, truth and wisdom and keeps it for those who seek.

5. **Redirection**: No matter how far off the path you get He can correct your direction for you.

6. **Listening**: God loves the sound of your voice. You're His child.

7. **Wealth**: God is not lacking. How can you believe Him for finances if He is poor?

8. **Peace**: When I spend time with Him I become more peaceful.

9. **Protection**: People pray when they get afraid.

10. **Health**: People pray when they get sick.

11. **Imagination**: Every night the sunset is different but has the same elements.

12. **Promotion**: Every promotion comes from God. All power and authority.

Choose three of the listed characteristics of God and describe how connecting with these traits could bring positive change in your life?

1. Attribute: _____ Change:_____

2. Attribute: _____ Change:_____

3. Attribute: _____ Change:_____

F YOU ARE IN THIS type of situation—one in which you need help but you are rejecting God—you are hearing two voices. One is compelling, drawing you toward God and the other is pushing you to stay in your addiction to numb the pain. The open invitation to try to find a relationship with God is on one side and the draw of your addiction is on the other side. You are standing between the two trying to figure out which way to go. Are you going to die in your addiction, or is something going to happen that is going to turn you around?

_____

_____

_____

_____

_____

_____

_____

_____

_____

_____

_____

_____

_____

_____

_____

_____

_____

David Sutton

Step # 4 Made a searching and fearless moral inventory of ourselves.

PRINCIPLE: *COURAGE*

WELCOME TO YOUR NEW LIFE

People of courage!

TWO THINGS I MUST CONSIDER ABOUT THE PAST

I T PROBABLY DIDN'T HAPPEN LIKE I remember it. It probably doesn't matter that much.

The recovery processes are entered into because of grace, not to earn grace. When we begin to do the activity of the steps there is a possibility that we would begin to believe that we need to do this to earn grace. We are able to take this inventory because of grace not to gain grace.

God is love. Everyone seems to like that message. We may or may not believe it down inside, however it is the message of the day, particularly in our society. It seems clear that God loves us. But there is another side to this matter. The love message without justice will always be imbalanced.

There needs to be a balance between love and justice. It is important not to approach your recovery with a haphazard manner. Thinking that there are no lasting consequences to behaviors, now that we have stopped our active addiction, is not the case. The idea that everything is operated by random occurrence relieves us of responsibility, past and present.

To believe that God will not judge wrongdoing is the opiate that allows us to continue in error believing that there is no consequence. A verse that describes it well is:

Ecclesiastes 8:11 "because the sentence of an evil deed is not carried out quickly…"

We don't see an immediate result of our action and we begin to believe that we can once again get away with wrong behavior. But this is really not true.

Numbers 32:23 "Be sure your sin will find you out."

Made a fearless and searching moral inventory of ourselves. This process is in many ways about making a series of commitments. When you think of what you are willing to make a commitment to ask yourself the following questions:

1.   What is one thing I am willing to commit to, in order to stay
       sober, not only physically, but emotionally as well?

_____

2. Am I ready to commit to change both internal and external things in order to grow in a new lifestyle? _____Yes _____No

If your answer is yes, describe one of each:

Internal: _____ External: _____

If no, the question is why not? _____

3. Will I make a commitment to identify who I have become and who I would like to be? _____Yes _____No

Identify one characteristic you want to change and what would it be changed to?

_____

_____

4. I am making a commitment to what I want to be. Name three things you would like to become.

a. _____

b. _____

c. _____

5. What sacrifices am I willing to commit to make this transition? Name three.

a. _____

b. _____

c. _____

6. What is it that I believe enough in, that I am willing to make a lifestyle change, to make it part of my belief system?

_____

_____

David Sutton

7. Am I committed to give up the one destructive thing, my drug of choice, to get back everything, the rest of my life? _____Yes _____No

Sobriety without an inventory has many negative characteristics. Choose which of the following behavioral traits you can see in your life.

Scattered	Yes	No
Distorted	Yes	No
Exaggerated	Yes	No
Extreme	Yes	No
Always / never	Yes	No
Uncertain	Yes	No
Confusing	Yes	No
Reactionary	Yes	No

Characteristic: _____

Example: _____

"IF FAITH IS THE OPPOSITE OF FEAR, THEN COURAGE IS THE ANTIDOTE"

1. *Courage is an active decision to respond in a productive way to fear.*

2. *Courage is not backing down when you feel like running.*

3. *Courage is getting up just one more time than I have been knocked down.*

4. *Courage is not surrendering when you feel hopeless.*

5. *Courage isn't the absence of fear in my life it's doing something in spite of the fears.*

6. *Courage is walking into the fear.*

7. *Courage is taking action in the face of danger, calamity or discouragement.*

Select two of the descriptions of courage listed and describe how you can apply them in your life.

Number _____ _____

Number _____ _____

N ANALYZING FEAR, REMEMBER THAT fact and truth are not the same thing, just as experiences and meanings are not identical. For example, the experiences you have may be different than the meanings you attach to them. In other words, meaning is the interpretation of your experience, and this is a key point in your inventory. It's not what you experienced so much as what you perceived you experienced. And most likely your perception was and still is effected by low self esteem, low self worth, low self image, as well as the memories of all of your failures and shortcomings.

_____

_____

_____

_____

_____

_____

_____

_____

_____

_____

_____

_____

_____

_____

_____

_____

_____

_____

_____

David Sutton

Step # 5 Admitted to God, ourselves and to another human being, the exact nature of our wrongs.

PRINCIPLE: *INTEGRITY*

WELCOME TO YOUR NEW LIFE

Integrity minded people!

Admitting to God: Admitting to myself:
Admitting to another person:

ADMITTING THAT WE ARE WRONG in even one small issue is sometimes very difficult. To admit that we have been wrong in the way we have lived our lives, the values we have held and the way we have treated others, is beyond that which we can ever do on our own strength. Asking God to help us through this task is the only way we will fulfill it. This asking is the perfect place to begin. Not only are we asking for help, but we can at the same time move forward into our confession before Him.

In order to admit to God

God must be...

God must be believed...

God must be trusted...

God must be listening...

God must be interested...

God must be understanding...

God must be responding...

God must be forgiving...

God must be repairing...

God must be planning...

God must be OK with it all...

God must be God...

God must be...

There are many who hold to the belief that I don't need to confess anything to anybody just to God. God who hears and knows all things will in His mercy forgive me and that will resolve it. This, for as far as it goes, is fine. God does hear and forgive. If it were simply forgiveness we were trying to achieve in the working of this step, the step wouldn't be necessary. If you found God and surrendered to Him, in this process, you received forgiveness at that point. If you don't feel that He has forgiven you, perhaps you're as surrendered as you think. However, forgiveness is not the point or purpose of this step.

This clearly deals with accountability to others. "Confess your faults one to another, and pray one for the other, that you may be healed." (James 5:16) Many people have fallen back to their old lifestyle of addiction, because their life lacked accountability. This concept is something quite foreign to those caught up in a life of self-centered addictions. In fact the highest levels of energy normally expended by a person active in compulsive behaviors were focused on "the great cover up." Most majored in hiding who we were, what we were doing, and how we felt and thought. Accountability to someone for our behavior becomes vital in exposing the depth that our addiction had fallen to.

Integrity is the principle we are dealing with. Integrity is easiest to see in the light of our character and reputation. A person's reputation is the part of them that everyone sees. Fortunes are spent and lifetimes have been invested in the building of one's reputation. What will people think or say about me that is the question. We all desire to have a good reputation. In fact the Bible admonishes us that "a good name is to be chosen rather than great riches." The problem is found in the deception of pretending to be something or somebody that you are not. When my reputation becomes what I want people to believe that I am and not who I really am; therein lies the problem.

My character is who I am when no one is around. The true heart of a man is his character. When my character and my reputation are the same, I am then walking in integrity. When the two are different then there is a breach in this integrity, and I am no longer able to live honestly. This loss of honest living is first to God, then to myself and ultimately to others. To regain integrity I must become accountable in all areas.

Suffice it to say if I am honest with myself and not before God it will have a negative result in my relationship with Him. If I am honest with just me and God and not people, the negative effect will be upon my personal relationships with others. There are two purposes of this step:

- ✓ First is to clear up the past and gain integrity.

- ✓ Second is less conspicuous, but equally important. It is the acknowledgment of the need for ongoing accountability, and grasping integrity as a lifestyle.

It was quite easy to see all of the pain I had caused others. Taking a closer, deeper look made it obvious that much of what I was going through was fostered out of issues of being ashamed. Many episodes of others taking advantage of me, came to mind. The issues of shame were almost too great to deal with. Thank God for His mercy. The chronology of the step was the very thing that made it work so well. Once I was open before God, the other parts didn't seem so hard.

David Sutton

A major step in gaining life integrity is admitting to another person, both your wrong behaviors and selfish motives. Confession creates a clear, necessary connection to others. When you find you are not connected to others it is the first sign of the lack of accountability and the loss of integrity.

So ask yourself the following questions:

1.   When was the last time you found yourself in isolation?

_____

_____

What started it?

_____

_____

2.   Do you see your life moving toward people or away from people?

_____

3.   Do you desire to have more friends in your life? _____Yes _____No

If yes, what is one thing you can currently do to make this connection?

_____

If no, why not?

_____

4.   Have any of the people you look to for help, pointed out
that you are isolating? _____Yes _____No

5.   Do you believe what they are saying? _____Yes _____No

6.   Is there any time that you choose to isolate and avoid people? _____Yes _____No

When and on what occasions?

_____

_____

7. How has isolation cost you monetarily?

    _____

8. Why do you feel more comfortable alone?

    _____

    How can you change this?

    _____

9. Are you willing to allow others to speak into your life? _____Yes _____No

    Give an example:

    _____

10. What is one thing you are willing to do to stay connected to other people?

    _____

ACCOUNTABILITY REQUIRES:

1. Challenge

2. Confrontation

3. Correction

4. Consequences

5. Closure

Which of the following dimensions of accountability can you identify in your personal connection to others?

Challenge: _____Yes _____No

What were you challenged about?

_____

_____

Confrontation: _____Yes _____No

Who were you confronted by?

_____

_____

Correction: _____Yes _____No

What was the correction you received?

_____

_____

Consequence: _____Yes _____No

How was the consequence effective?

_____

_____

Closure: _____Yes _____No

Did you find closure to what you were challenged about? _____

_____

_____

ACCOUNTABILITY PROVIDES:

1. Connection with the Real You

2. Consistent Contact (we based recovery)

3. Protection from Unrealistic Choices Decisions (protection from fantasy)

4. Solution Based Focus

5. Favor and Opportunity

6. Protection from Self-sabotage

7. Training for Assisting Others

Select two of the items that accountability provides from those listed and describe how they apply to you.

1. _____

   _____

   _____

   _____

   _____

2. _____

   _____

   _____

   _____

   _____

THIS IS THE SOUL CLEANSING step. You recognize that deep inside of your soul there is some kind of sickness, something that just never feels quite right. You don't feel comfortable in your own skin when you walk into a room, for example. There is something wrong on the inside and you need to find integrity and make a change..

_____

_____

_____

_____

_____

_____

_____

_____

_____

_____

_____

_____

_____

_____

_____

_____

_____

_____

_____

_____

_____

David Sutton

Step # 6 Were entirely ready to have God remove all of these character defects.

PRINCIPLE: *WILLINGNESS*

WELCOME TO YOUR NEW LIFE

People of a willing heart!

THE MOST REVEALING QUESTION THAT I have ever found to ask someone who is seeking help is, "What are you willing to do to get better?" The responses are of course infinite. There is one reply that says it all when it comes to willingness; that is a single word answer, "anything!"

The ultimate sign of a person who is truly ready to make a life change, is that they are ready to do anything that it takes to find recovery. Even for those who seem at first eager to recover, when faced with the challenge of taking action and making changes that are foreign to how they have lived, might shy away. But the person, who has concluded that they will do anything and everything it takes, is on their way to total life renewal.

This describes those who, that in their heart, want nothing less than to find total freedom from their addiction. The desire to get free moves from a passive wanting or hoping, into an active exercise of faith in God. This willingness of the heart, when empowered by God, activates the change. In order to see the fulfillment of this change in my life, I must be free from the old behavior patterns that have haunted me. When we ask with a right heart attitude, God will remove from us everything that has caused us to remain in the state of disfunction. This surrender is really about letting go of the self serving life. Once genuine surrender takes place, we begin to live to please God, family and others.

Many in this state of transition will only become partially ready. They desire that God would remove the things from their life, that appear to be bringing a negative result. However many have behaviors and compulsions that they purposefully retain, thinking that they can still derive some selfish pleasure from them. They imagine that somehow they can enjoy the "pleasures of sin for a season," without reaping any subsequent fallout. This is a fallacy that has lead many to relapse again and again.

Where does this willingness to let go come from? Only from God. God not only can remove the defects of character, He can also remove the resistance in your heart to let go of the wrong things. If you are at a point that you want to change, but for some reason can't let go, you can find a starting place. If you are aware that you have often made many promises to yourself and have not been able to keep promises to you, but you might just be ready to try something different. Simply pray for the "willingness to be willing."

For some this may sound redundant, but for those that know that their heart is deceitful will, with a good measure of success, try this simple prayer. A verse that describes this so well is

II Corinthians 8:3 "...and beyond their power they were willing of themselves." Those who have found God's intervention in dramatic ways know that He is able to do well beyond anything that we can accomplish on our own strength. Just as long as we are open to try, He will always come through.

Willingness is normally limited to our understanding, our abilities and presenting opportunity. When our choice (our will) is blended with surrender (to God) we can bypass the human condition and parameters."

The root word of willingness is will. Free will is not defined by what I feel but by what I believe. Regarding our will, there are two immutable truths about free will: God will never override your exercise of it and the minute you ask God to empower free will, he does. It is your free will and your life and God cares about it. We're defined by what we believe not what we feel. We no longer have to succumb to emotions, so exercise of free will is simpler because decisions are not based on circumstances or popular opinion.

The journey to willingness may be a laborious thing at the beginning, however it doesn't have to remain difficult. There comes a time in most of those moving through recovery, that we fall in love with the process. This is willingness on an entirely different level. The word to describe this higher level is alacrity (uh-**lak**-ri-tee) cheerful readiness, promptness, or willingness: no longer a dreadful doing, but an energized anticipation.

When you consider your level of willingness to actually change there are some immediate issues that will block your progress. So consider each of the following and how it applies.

1. **The fear of change.** You're not sure what you will be like if you change. What is the specific change that you are holding on to or have not addressed?

    _____

2. **Un-forgiveness.** Do I see people in my life that I still have un-forgiveness toward? Who are you willing to forgive, that you previously refused to consider?

    _____

    What is the offense?

    _____

3. **Denial.** This is being unwilling or unable to see anything wrong. Thinking the area that needs to change is just a personality trait you were born with. Identify one area of your life that you have been in denial about.

    _____

4. **A sense of inadequacy.** Are you still struggling with a feeling of inadequacy and not measuring up? _____Yes _____No

If yes, in what way?

_____

5. **Lack of knowledge.** Describe an area of your life that you are not sure how to completely let go?

_____

6. **Other people's influence.** Has someone convinced you that you cannot change because they haven't?

Who?

_____

How?

_____

7. **The quick fix mentality.** We want to feel good right now, not waiting for the results of hard work. What instant feel good thing are you trying to hold on to?

_____

8. **Lack of faith.** If you don't believe that the change will come or that the change will last, that is a faith failure. What is one area that I need to increase my faith?

_____

9. **Procrastination.** Putting off the activity involved to make change. What is one thing you have put off that would provide changes to come?

_____

10. **Pride.** A pride-full attitude. How has pride blocked my progress?

_____

All change requires an act of our free will. Willingness is openness, honesty, determination, planning, choosing and doing.

1. **What choices have you been willing to make to stay sober?**

Pray more often.	**Yes**	**No**
Abstain from alcohol.	**Yes**	**No**
Go to meetings.	**Yes**	**No**
Call an accountability person.	**Yes**	**No**
Form a relationship with God.	**Yes**	**No**
Read about change.	**Yes**	**No**
Are you willing to ask, "what does it take?"	**Yes**	**No**

2. **Are you willing to stay away from:**

   ☐ **Unhealthy people - family, old friends**

   ☐ **Chaotic places - party places, scary, mind places**

   ☐ **Destructive things - activities, food**

Select one from the group above and describe how you will do this.

_____

_____

3. **Are you willing to get near to:**

   ☐ **Spiritual people - recovery people, church people**

   ☐ **Peaceful places - the beach, meetings**

   ☐ **Constructive things - exercise, education**

Select one from the group above and describe how you will do this.

_____

_____

4. **Are you willing to plan for:**

☐ **Emergencies - health, finance**

☐ **Disappointments - betrayal, prepared for a day not years**

☐ **Success - money, relationship**

Select one from the group above and describe how you will do this.

_____

_____

The crux of our problem as people in recovery is multidimensional. We often operate in one or more of the following characteristics:

Extreme Rebellion: Revolt, indifference and unresponsiveness

Fierce Independence: Self-government, autonomy, sovereignty

Radical Self-reliance: Self determination, self rule

Intense Isolation: Silence, loneliness, inverted thinking

All of these attitudes describe internal posturing. Each constitutes an internal state that we cannot hear the voice of our conscience. Select two of the traits listed above and describe how they apply to you.

1. _____

_____

2. _____

_____

GOD CARES ABOUT YOU, AND He wants you to know that he cares about you. He has a plan for your life. Did you know that? He has a purpose and a destiny for your life. You weren't born by mistake in this life to do nothing. God did not intend for you to end up as an alcoholic or addict and screw up your life. Rest assured that God has something better for you. If he didn't then He would not have given you a pathway or process so that you could get out of this mess. He didn't rescue you from drowning in the ocean to beat you up on the beach.

_____

_____

_____

_____

_____

_____

_____

_____

_____

_____

_____

_____

_____

_____

_____

_____

David Sutton

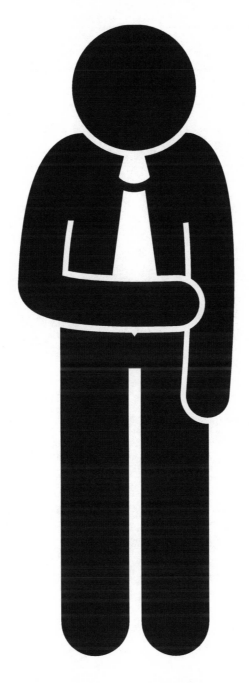

Step # 7 Humbly ask him to remove our shortcomings.

PRINCIPLE: *HUMILITY*

WELCOME TO YOUR NEW LIFE

People of a Humble Manner!

A PERSON WHO HUMBLES THEMSELF, WILL keep them self from being humiliated later. This process of humbling oneself is the perfect antidote to pride. In the words of an old proverb, "A man's pride shall bring him low, but honor shall uphold the humble in spirit." There are times that humility falls on a life like a cloak and covers you over. The struggle to maintain some semblance of order remains, however, there comes a point that the person's life will never be the same. The event is so great and the impact so overpowering that the impact is permanent.

There are basically two pathways to accessing humility. The first is a pathway of difficulty that comes in two basic forms, both tragedy and personal failure. We are all familiar and most have experienced the path of personal failures. The struggle to maintain gainful employment, failed marriages, wayward children, financial blunders and the list goes on ad infinitum. Tragedy brings about the same humbling effect, however is not usually connected to the guilt and remorse found in personal failure.

In recent years we have seen an escalation in the devastating effects of violent weather conditions. In the aftermath we find most people have been humbled from not only the wreckage, but the loss of control in their lives. Sometimes losing someone close to us in death can be humbling, whether by sickness or accidental death.

An area that I have found personally, that brings this process to my life, that seems to be somewhat of a blend of both is my failed efforts to help someone. Those who have gone back to addiction, prison or even premature death, seems to resonate with devastating results on everyone. Interesting, as the person trying to help, it always places a clear focus on my human fallibility.

While the pathway of difficulty seems to be well traveled on the road to finding a humble place in one's heart, there is another way; it is the pathway of connection. Let me describe how these play out.

The first connection is to people of greatness. I have met many great leaders, scholars and even performers that carried with them a persona of excellence. The power, influence and authority they carry set them apart. The level of their development and their refined manner, made it a privilege just to spend time with them.

The next connection in the pathway is that of gifts given into my life. There have been many occasions that people have touched my life with gifts. While these certainly include material gifts, often the best gift is that of someone devoting their time and energy into my personal life. I've found that receiving from others requires a humble heart and in turn creates a greater level of humility by simply experiencing charity.

The place of honor can produce either humility or pride. Mostly it depends on the recipient. Those who find that the recognition of their personal achievement, was largely dependent on the assistance and contribution of others, will most often find receiving the place of honor, a humbling experience. The person who feels that they made it on their own, with no need for help from others, will when honored, become more filled with self-centered pride.

The final connection I cannot fail to mention is the God connection. Human fallibility in the shadow of an infinite God, will humble even the most rigid of conditions in the human heart. Both in the realization of God's providence and in the answers to prayers offered from the weakness of human condition, hearts are humbled. If you find this connection difficult the answer comes by way of spending time, development of communication with God. No relationship human or Divine comes without the investment of time.

The key to successfully working this step is in the very first word. For many they "humbly demand" that God do this or God do that. It was as though it was in their heart that God was at their beckon call. That somehow they could just tell Him what to do and He would have to respond. It doesn't work quite that way. If you remove the word "humbly" from this step, the remainder of the step is simply a prayer, a process of asking.

This type of asking prayer is what is known as a "petition." The word petition is a formal request, presented to an authority or power, for a change in way or order of things. The dictionary even describes it as begging. This wording is commonly seen in the legal system. Petitions are presented to a court or a judge to bring about change. Often the verbiage is presented in a fashion that says something like:

"Your Honor, We the petitioners pray that...". This encapsulates the entire feel of this "humbly asking" process.

Consider the process of grasping the principle of humility. The following represent either the pathway of difficulty or the path of connection. Mark each event with either the word difficulty or connection.

1. Inheriting a lot of money. _____

2. Working a program of recovery. _____

3. Divorcing your spouse. _____

4. Having a child join the military. _____

5. Starting a new business. _____

6. Getting clean and sober. _____

7. Starting a new romance. _____

8. Being terminated from work. _____

9. Getting a speeding ticket. _____

It is easy to spot pride in others, not so easy in us. Pride that is seen in others may be a reflection of our own mess. Are you carrying the message or just the mess? **Which of the following traits can you identify in yourself as pride-full?**

Perpetually late	Yes	No
Constant need to help others	Yes	No
Disrespect toward authority	Yes	No
Uncomfortable in receiving compliments	Yes	No
Making assumptions	Yes	No
Telling others what to do	Yes	No
Talking about your problems	Yes	No
Know it all attitude	Yes	No
Inability to listen to others without cutting them off	Yes	No

Select two of the traits you answered yes to as pride-full conditions in your life and describe how you could change them.

1. _____

_____

2. _____

_____

HUMILITY IS NOTHING BUT THE disappearance of self and the realization that God is all. God is either everything or He is nothing. In other words, either there is a God or there isn't a God. I was told early on, "There is a God and it's not you!" Today, I believe that. Humility is about giving up self reliance. At the core of the dilemma, at the core of this thing called addiction, is selfishness, self centeredness, self will, and this self life is destructive.

_____

_____

_____

_____

_____

_____

_____

_____

_____

_____

_____

_____

_____

_____

_____

_____

_____

_____

David Sutton

David Sutton

Step # 8 Made a list of all persons we have harmed, and became willing to make amends to them all.

PRINCIPLE: *BROTHERLY LOVE*

WELCOME TO YOUR NEW LIFE

People Who Love!

FOR THOSE WHO HAVE APPROACHED this life evaluation with any degree of self-honesty, it shouldn't be too difficult to assess the destruction that has come to your life from your behavior, attitudes and choices. Clearly this extends to individuals you've been associated with, especially those immediately around you. Seeing who we have harmed and identifying the need to make an honest attempt to rectify the situation is essential. However, identifying the wrong and taking action to correct it, may be two different subjects.

When making up this list it should be foremost in your mind, that the people that you damaged were victims. Does that mean that they were completely innocent of any wrongdoing? No, not necessarily. However it does point to the reality that your behavior was not acceptable, and some of their conduct may have been in response to your actions. You will never bridge broken relationships, if you are still attempting to put the blame on someone else. Those who have been in a lifestyle of covering their behavior will tend to automatically place the blame on people, places or things.

People coming out of an addictive behavior deserve a second chance. It is possible this opportunity is the result of the prayers of those who you were hurting, who were praying for God's intervention, that gave you this grace. Likely it was God's plan and mercy that you found your way out of addiction. To surmise that you are deserving, or you can excuse yourself for any of the things that went on, will open the door for you to begin justifying your actions.

Having identified those you have damaged, be careful not to entertain the thought that they somehow deserved it and you owe them nothing. On the other hand, if your indebtedness to them seems insurmountable, don't shy away from adding them to the list. The thought may come that you can never find resolve. This is an exercise in identifying where you have caused harm.

The level of relationship will drastically affect the level of reconciliation necessary. A former spouse or your children will certainly be a higher priority to resolve with, than a casual business acquaintance. Some relationships will appear far more complicated to ever repair than others. Measure carefully, and proceed boldly; knowing you are in God's will. No harm will come to those who are attempting to do His will. That is the safest place in life to ever be; the center of God's will.

Review the following questions as your considering formulating a list of those you owe an amends to:

1. When did I first become aware my actions were negatively affecting others? Give an example:

   _____

   _____

2. Describe one repetitive behavior that caused problems with multiple people.

   _____

   _____

3. Are you ready to repair any damage you caused?_____Yes _____No

   What is one situation are you not willing to address?

   _____

   _____

4. Do any of your actions seem warranted?_____Yes _____No If yes, Give an example:

   _____

   _____

5. Is there any person you refuse to reconsider? _____Yes _____No If yes, who and why?

   _____

   _____

6. Has fear caused me to procrastinate and put off this process? _____Yes _____No

   What specific fear are you experiencing?

   _____

   _____

7.   Why is it important to identify everyone I have harmed?

   _____

   _____

WHAT IS UNCONDITIONAL LOVE?

There are many characteristics of a person who demonstrates genuine love for others. Listed below are the characteristics of love. Identify the ones that you see in your own life and actions.

Which of these traits can you identify in yourself?

DO I PUT UP WITH OTHERS FAULTS?	Yes	No
AM I KIND TO OTHERS?	Yes	No
AM I MEAN TOWARD OTHERS?	Yes	No
DO I ENVY OTHERS?	Yes	No
DO I BRAG?	Yes	No
AM I TEACHABLE?	Yes	No
DO I SEE LOVE AND SEX AS THE SAME THING?	Yes	No
AM I SELFISH?	Yes	No
AM I EASILY PROVOKED?	Yes	No
DO I THINK WRONG OF OTHERS?	Yes	No
DO I CELEBRATE OTHERS FAILURES?	Yes	No
DO I CELEBRATE THINGS THAT ARE HONEST?	Yes	No

Select two of the traits listed and describe how they apply to your life.

1.   _____

   _____

2.   _____

   _____

THERE IS NOTHING MORE HUMBLING than walking into the process of looking headlong at all the people that you have harmed. And trust me, everybody who has suffered from an addiction has harmed somebody at some point. When I started making my list it was short. It was what came immediately to mind and it was short because I was lazy. However, I needed to begin to walk back through my life and look at everybody I actually harmed when I was high, in the times that I was planning on getting high, when I was working on my next drunk, or trying to get sober so that I could go back out again. It was all about me and my selfishness. At that point in my life I can assure you there was nobody who came into my path who was not damaged by my behaviors—hurt by my words, deeds, thought processes, profane language, etc.

_____

_____

_____

_____

_____

_____

_____

_____

_____

_____

_____

_____

_____

_____

_____

David Sutton

Step # 9 Make direct amends wherever possible, except when to do so would injure them or others.

PRINCIPLE: *DISCIPLINE*

WELCOME TO YOUR NEW LIFE

Disciplined people!

THE VERY PROCESS OF GOING to others and exposing yourself as a phony, an abuser or self centered, can stir up apprehension in the average heart. It is probably the furthest thing from your natural inclinations as you can find. That is why the principle of discipline fits so well with this process. The dictionary describes discipline as, "bringing to a state of order and obedience, by training and control." This is a process that everyone who as ever achieved any appreciable goals or achievements knows well.

The participants in the Olympic Games spend years going over and over the same moves until they have perfected them. After some time they begin to find that their body will perform much of this without the necessity of a focused thought. Their thought processes can then move to the higher level of perfecting these various athletic maneuvers. This does not happen the first time they do it, but requires hundreds of hours of practice. From the state of their limited beginnings to world class perfection, requires hours of diligent dedication to their task.

In the same manner, this process of going to others and making right the wrong will at first feel uncomfortable and awkward. However, after you have begun the task it will become easier than you would have imagined. Will it ever become effortless or comfortable? Probably not. But the truth of the matter is that the impact this will have in your life, and those you are reconciling with, will for the most part be favorable. The design of this step is to get you to resolve the difficulties of the past. The process will allow you to develop the skills necessary to embrace as a lifestyle, this method of keeping the slate clean with those around you.

Discipline is action that is motivated from within. Discipline says, try it this way, it works; or we've done it like this and we have found good results. The process of discipline is not doing big things and moving on to something else. Discipline is somewhat of the opposite. It is doing small things well with a suitable amount of frequency, to produce the desired results.

Short term sustainable goals when achieved, produce long term results.

The greatest exercise in discipline is "wanting to," "not having to." We may begin with duty but desire should supplant duty. The task will always seem to be an insurmountable task, until we formulate the concept of discipline. In the momentary difficulty of the task at hand, we set our sights on the final result. In discipline, the ultimate goal gets us past the hard areas. When we feel like quitting and are in the thoughts of "I just can't do this anymore," the need to adjust our thoughts toward our objective will become the crucial turning point.

If we fix our sights on the ultimate goal; the final result will take us temporarily out of the moment. Out of the moment of maybe...

- ✓ Just long enough to, pass the need to quit.

- ✓ Just long enough to, find the internal fortitude to continue on.

- ✓ Just long enough to, move from an attitude of self pity to the strengthening place of being grateful.

- ✓ Just long enough to, see we are still in the running if we continue.

With a disciplined approach, there will not be someone checking up on you to see if you have followed through with working these steps. It may be that a loving sponsor or spouse might ask what step are you on, or have you have done your steps? But the truth of the matter is nobody is keeping score, just you.

It probably will cost you something to right the wrong. The willingness to make amends will come however, if you will take the responsibility for your behavior. You may identify in advance some things that you can do to restore the damage. First you must face the person and make it known what your intentions are. Only then will you begin to see what can be done to find reconciliation.

While an apology is fine, and a wonderful starting point, but be sure to ask the person what you can do to make right the wrong. Their idea may be much different than yours. You may find that they will just say forget it, and forgive you; or it may be that they won't even talk to you. Nevertheless, for you to make a concerted effort to find a remedy will be necessary.

When you think of making amends start by asking yourself the following questions:

1. When did I last engage in behavior that was harmful to others?

    _____

    _____

2. Do I routinely see any of those I owe amends to? _____Yes _____No

    If yes, who? _____and where? _____

3. What do you want see happen as a result of your amends?

_____

_____

4. Do any of the people you need to reconcile with refuse to
   have contact with you? _____Yes _____No

   If yes who and why?

   _____

   _____

5. If you answered yes to the previous question, what could you do to correct the situation?

   _____

   _____

6. Have any of the listed people died or disappeared? _____Yes _____No

   If yes, who? _____

7. Am I putting off making amends to anyone? _____Yes _____No

   If yes, who and why?

   _____

   _____

8. Are you willing to go to any lengths to make these amends? _____Yes _____No

   If your answer is no, give a description of why you are resistant.

   _____

   _____

9. Will I do the things I am asked to do to right the wrongs? _____Yes _____No

    If no, what won't you do and why?

    _____

    _____

Discipline Requires

1. **Focus and Purpose**: the reason for doing anything repeatedly.
    Describe your purpose in making amends.

    _____

    _____

2. **Routine and Consistency**: finding a place, time and routine.
    How will you insure a consistent effort.

    _____

    _____

3. **Goals and Results**: small enough increments to measure effectively.
    List 3 goals you can set to insure this process.

    _____

    _____

    _____

4. **Faith and Encouragement**: self encouragement is sometimes necessary, because others
    may fail to encourage when it's needed. Write a statement of self encouragement.

    _____

    _____

5. **Measure and Redefining**: once small goals are met a reset is necessary. How will you measure your results and reestablish your goals.

_____

_____

6. **Contentment and Satisfaction**: Be happy with short your term successes! Describe two areas of your progress that you are either contented with or have found satisfaction in.

_____

_____

F YOU BECAME WILLING TO identify those you harmed, you now have the potential and know how to forgive other people. Remember you said you were willing to make it right with them all. You made a decision on the inside that nobody owes you anything. When I got into the position where I felt as if nobody owed me anything,…

_____

_____

_____

_____

_____

_____

_____

_____

_____

_____

_____

_____

_____

_____

_____

_____

_____

David Sutton

Step # 10 Continued to take personal inventory and when we were wrong promptly admitted it.

PRINCIPAL: *PERSEVERANCE*

WELCOME TO YOUR NEW LIFE

Persistent people!

To CONTINUE TO TAKE A personal inventory two things must occur. You must have taken an inventory and by necessity are still working on it. You can quickly see the logic in the language of this process. It's a continuation of the inventory began in the earlier parts of your journey.

My inventory may include input from others, but the inventory is still mine. I listen to what people say and apply the things that will cause me to grow spiritually. But it is still my choice. Continuing in a lifestyle inventory is substantively learning how to listen and observe. We are measuring what to hang on to and what to let go of. Both those things I need, and those I don't want to include in my life. It is in the listening that you identify the things that will help you grow and the things that will take you back out. If you will take the time to identify the differences, you won't have to start over again. Start your inventory now, so that you don't need to restart your sobriety later. If you don't change, your sobriety date will.

The ongoing inventory is the way we move the recovery process from head knowledge to our heart knowledge. Perseverance is really about moving knowledge of recovery from your head into your heart. When it remains as head knowledge, complacency will follow. People who get complacent will likely return to old behaviors. Going to meetings, making the phone call, stepping up when you don't feel it and continuing when everything is upside down; this is perseverance.

The head informs; the heart transforms. Transformation occurs first in the heart. Remember recovery is not an activity; it's a lifestyle. Head knowledge that is not established in the heart, produces superficial sobriety. With it comes more guilt, confusion and more expanded conflict with others. Knowledge by itself will not transform your life. Transformation requires God's power. To access true transformation requires both Divine revelation of our life and God's power to change it.

There are multiple parts to our daily inventory. Physical, emotional, relational conditions and spiritual, are all in your inventory.

If the focus of your personal inventory is your physical being, make sure you understand how your body functions and how it reveals what it needs. If you feel thirsty, it has nothing to do with needing alcohol, perhaps you simply need a big drink of water. If your hungry, inventory when you ate last. Learn how to properly nourish your body and choosing to make the healthy choices, is the best way to address hunger. If you're tired look at your sleep patterns.

The craving your experiencing might not be triggered by a physical need. Often it is the byproduct of an emotional deficiency. When you feel unsettled, agitated or lack peace, take an on-the-spot emotional inventory. Addicts don't pick up their drug of choice because they want to ruin their lives, but because they want to change the way they feel. What is it that you are feeling? At any point in the day you should be able to stop and measure what you are feeling. The inventory is not an event, but is a process.

Inventory your relationships, too. Be persistent in your self evaluation to see if you are isolating again. Look at what meaningful relationships you're in. Every relationship, both human and Divine requires the investment of energy and time. Are you spending time with the people that are truly important. Reviewing the relationships that are not healthy, is an equally important function. Some relationships are draining, time consuming and toxic. Separating yourself from such just might save your life.

Our inventory must always include the spiritual aspects of our life. Are you consistently praying? Studying? Is your faith growing? Are you still passionate? Passions and affections are founded in our beliefs. Passions and affections are central to, and a byproduct of, our belief system. When these are set on the wrong things it will destroy faith and the result will be nothing but destruction. I am not defined by what I feel. I am defined by what I believe. What I believe makes me who I am. So too much focus on a wrong belief can destroy who I am.

There is a school of thought that says knowledge is power. It is as far as it goes. However knowledge is often limited and constrained to one area of life. They may be an expert in their field, but if they can't stay sober what good is the knowledge? And we know people who can quote the text but have no power to stay away from the first drink. Knowledge has both moral quality and power. When it's used well, it has the capacity to shape character.

The two things that will most affect your life in the next 5 years, are the books you read and the people you meet. Consider the following questions regarding your daily inventory:

1.   In general what are you feeding your mind? (Reading, Facebook, News, politics, sports, etc.)

   _____

   _____

2.   What type of books, magazines, media ideas engage you and why? Name two.

   _____

   _____

3.   What amount of time do you spend weekly feeding your mind?

_____

4. Do you have any goals in development of your intellect? _____Yes _____No

   Describe:

   _____

   _____

5. Who are you meeting and connecting with?

   _____

   _____

6. Who is speaking into your life?

   _____

   _____

7. What person would you like to meet this year and why?

   _____

   _____

8. Did I speak to anyone today in a mean or sarcastic way? Who? _____

   What did I say?

   _____

   _____

9. Do I need to go back and correct this? _____Yes _____No

   Were my attitudes positive or negative? _____ Give an example:

   _____

10.   What was my predominate feeling today? _____

11.   Did I want my own way without considering the impact on others? _____Yes _____No

      Give an example:

      _____

      _____

12.   Have I made a quality effort to do something nice or special for someone else?
      Who? _____ What did you do?

      _____

      _____

13.   Did I spend prayer and meditation time today? Yes _____ No _____

14.   Describe a positive effort you took to build your spiritual life:

      _____

      _____

15.   Describe two ways your spiritual life has grown:

      1. _____

      2. _____

16.   What plan did I have, either positive or negative, that I failed to carry out?

      How did this affect me or others?

      _____

      _____

17. What am I supposed to be doing today that I can't or won't do? _____

18. Did I do the things necessary to stay free from my addiction today? _____Yes _____No

    One thing I did: _____

    One thing I failed to do:_____

All change demands self appraisal. The fact that I can identify failure in myself is progress. It is sometimes more difficult to see the positive. Which of the following traits can you identify in yourself?

Faithfulness	Yes	No
Purity of motives	Yes	No
Loyalty	Yes	No
Ambition	Yes	No
Kindness	Yes	No
Regard for others	Yes	No
Unselfishness	Yes	No
Balance	Yes	No

There are four basic absolutes necessary to find recovery:

Honesty – Purity – Unselfishness – Love

With these four absolutes, we can enter into an ongoing honest appraisal of our lives. Describe how each of these absolutes is effecting change or can apply in your inventory:

Honesty: _____

Purity: _____

Unselfishness: _____

Love: _____

HERE WE PERSISTENTLY, CONSISTENTLY WORK on all that we have done and continue to do. To take individual daily account of who we are and what we are doing, both good and bad. When we enter this process we can face our wrongs and acknowledge our failures. This critical step focuses on activating all of these principles into one process in your life that encompasses everything—the good, the bad, and the ugly. This is the place where you have to do the things that you really don't want to do to remain whole.

_____

_____

_____

_____

_____

_____

_____

_____

_____

_____

_____

_____

_____

_____

_____

_____

David Sutton

David Sutton

Step # 11 - Sought thru prayer and meditation to improve our conscious contact with God, as we understood Him, praying only for the knowledge of His will for us and the power to carry that out.

PRINCIPAL: AWARENESS OF GOD

WELCOME TO YOUR NEW LIFE

Spiritually Minded People!

THE PREREQUISITE FOR THIS STEP in your journey is a belief in God. If you don't believe in God, when you get to this point, not only won't it work, it simply can't. You will find no connection to God without an established belief in God. Your connection to God must have been established previously or there can be no awareness of God, let alone an "improved" conscious contact. To improve is to increase or upgrade. We improve something by replacing the old worn-out version with something better. There is a necessity for something to be in place originally, in order to improve on it.

There needs to be a connection made with God to expand upon. For most, this connection was with a first cry for help when you finally surrendered. You found yourself broken and asked for help from a power outside yourself. For most we didn't care what God was or looked like; we needed help. In the state of desperation it didn't matter. Only when we got feeling better did we begin to analyze, scrutinize and complain. We mostly connect to God in a crisis, only later we want to define God the way we would like God to be. If you have the power to create God in the form you would like, you must then, by reason, be more powerful than God. So if you create God, then God doesn't have all the power; it's your creation and you have the power not God. You must find God, the One with all power.

Some want to create a God with no rules. I wanted to stay sober but still do what I wanted, when I wanted, where I wanted, with whom and how often I wanted. But it did not work. I needed a God more powerful than myself.

Sought means seeking, looking, finding. It is not just a casual glance; it is more intensive. It is through Prayer and Meditation we improve our conscious awareness and connection with God. Some think prayer is talking to God and meditation is listening to God, but I disagree. Prayer is not a monolog or a speech. Prayer is a dialog wherein we talk to God and God talks to us. This actually happens when we take time out and make the occasion to pray a priority. Get quiet; turn off the cell phone, the TV and the tunes. Not trying to fit a little prayer into the rest of your life, but making it an important priority. If you do this the promise is that God will reveal more and your conscious awareness will improve.

God always reveals Himself to folks who take the time to seek him. You will have real guidance for life. It will be more than the guidance of judges, challenges of attorneys, encouragement from ministers, or anyone else who wants to tell you what you should be doing. You will have God's input. The easiest way we improve our conscious contact with God is by getting close to God, by investing our time and focus.

There are also a couple ideas about meditation in this general application I will touch on. Meditation is mostly designed to quiet the mind. I don't believe you can ever clear the mind of all thought through simple meditation. Actually in our application that is really not the goal. The better question to ask is what you meditate on? What strengthens your focus and helps keep you focused?

Early on most of our negative thinking revolves around obsessive thoughts. Fear driven, unproductive and primarily a self-centered thought life. Meditation is the opportunity to practice changing the general direction of your thinking. What do you think about most of the time? What are the ideas and plans you want to focus on and goals you desire to establish. If you don't deliberately adjust your thoughts, your mind wanders everywhere. You can capture your thoughts and break the inner vow of negative self-talk.

A final idea to consider. You can't steal recovery. You cannot grow spiritually without growing morally. You cannot be a thief and expect to become spiritually fit. You will not be able to stay sober. You will not grow spiritually and you will languish in the misery of this disease. Many alcoholics and addicts starve to death at the sobriety table. Not moving forward spiritually.

When you consider your spiritual life and spiritual growth, ask yourself the following questions:

1. When was the last time I scheduled time to pray and meditate? _____

    How much time did I spend?

    _____

2. Do I see my spiritual fitness as a priority? _____Yes _____No If not, why?

    _____

3. Do you desire to grow in your connection with God? _____Yes _____No

4. Do any of the people I associate with encourage my spiritual growth? _____Yes _____No

    Name one person who encourages your faith: _____

    Name one who distracts from your spiritual life: _____

5. Is there any behavior or activity in my life that keeps me from connecting with God? _____Yes _____No If your answer is yes, what is it?

_____

6. Has my spiritual growth been seen by others? _____Yes _____No

    By who? _____

    In what way? _____

7. Am I sure what I believe? _____Yes _____No

    What am I willing to do to establish what I believe and grow in my beliefs?

    _____

8. Am I willing to change to make the connection? _____Yes _____No

    If so in what way?

    _____

9. What will I commit to doing that will expand a quality spiritual life?

    _____

We are to pray for the knowledge of God's will and to be empowered to carry it out.

God's Will Reveals

1. **Who should be in my life**

2. **Desires both healthy and wrong**

3. **Flaws in my plans**

4. **What I need to work on**

5. **How to stay healthy**

6. **Dangerous situations**

7. **Operation of virtues**

God's Power Creates

1. **Freedom from craving**

2. **It produces peace in the middle of conflict and turmoil**

3. **Beyond our confidence we are competent**

4. **Establishes worthiness**

5. **Freedom from compulsive thought processes**

6. **Ability to connect with others**

7. **Sense of belonging**

8. **Feeling of competence—incapability goes away**

9. **Direction for your life**

10. **Ability to see life's beauty**

From the ideas presented above, describe one way God has revealed his will for your life and given you power to carry out his plan:

_____

_____

All spiritual growth comes out of application of basic principles. If I can identify these in my life or the areas that these basics are void, I can grow.

Which of these principles can you identify in your life?

Focus	Yes	No
Faith	Yes	No
Accountability	Yes	No
Connection	Yes	No
Honor	Yes	No
Purity	Yes	No
Compassion	Yes	No
Recognition	Yes	No

Select two of the principles listed and describe how they apply to you.

1. _____

   _____

   _____

2. _____

   _____

   _____

There has never been anyone who knew anything that would say find a God that you don't understand and stay that way. It's a God that you can know and begin to understand, and it's the God of your experience. Now is the time to address your conscious contact with God praying for the two most important things for your life. The knowledge of God's will and that He would empower you to move straightway into accomplishing His plan for your life.

_____

_____

_____

_____

_____

_____

_____

_____

_____

_____

_____

_____

_____

_____

_____

_____

_____

David Sutton

David Sutton

Step # 12 Having had a spiritual awakening as the result of these steps, we tried to carry this message to alcoholics, and to practice these principles in all our affairs.

PRINCIPLE: SERVICE TO OTHERS

WELCOME TO YOUR NEW LIFE

People helping people!

THE ESSENCE OF THIS "SPIRITUAL awakening" that has come to us by working through these steps is this; it's all a gift given to us, to give to others. Certainly we have been enlightened of God's love for us. And of course we have seen our mistakes, before and after. Without a doubt we are never going to be perfect. But in our journey we have realized that God in His infinite mercy made a way that in helping others, we become engaged, productive members of society.

The key to our own recovery and happiness can be found in reaching out to those still suffering. "... love each other just as I have loved you. No one has greater love than to give up one's life for one's friends." (John 15:12-13 CEB). It is somewhat of a built in insurance policy for permanent lasting recovery, the love of God expressed through us to others.

As you attempt to help others you are able, through the lens of others suffering, to see the pain and destruction of your old lifestyle. This is often enough to keep strengthening ones sobriety, but the principle goes beyond that. Regardless of what you give out of your life it will be returned back to you again. Not only it comes back to you, but it is multiplied. So it is with Recovery. The basics of your life, food, shelter, encouragement and unconditional love, will be met as you give to others in need. The more you give out, the more you receive back. It begins a cycle that once discovered, becomes lifestyle.

Many have never found this realization. Often their sobriety is lacking and they can easily be disillusioned. They have fixed their eyes on what they want, and not the needs of others. It has been said that it is a selfish program, but this is not accurate. The meaning is that you need to do whatever is necessary to stay free from your addiction. However it is generally understood that selfishness and self centered behavior is at the core of our addiction. If selfishness is the problem, then selfish behavior and attitudes, cannot be the answer.

There is a correlation between your ability to love and that which you have been forgiven of; a direct comparison to your own healing and your willingness to help others; the breaking of the self-centered thinking and openness to assist others in their recovery.

It goes without saying whom are critical and harsh in their view of others have often forgotten where they have come from. Certainly everyone has fallen short of God's mercy, but to those who have come from a low place, it is much easier to remember.

Helping others find recovery is the key to permanent lasting recovery. I am 100% successful with all of those that I reach out to. Even if none of them are sober, I am. If anyone should benefit from my attempts to help them, that is good. However the approach is this; if I will try to help others, God will keep me in a pathway of growth.

The Principle Approach Workbook

Anything worth doing is worth practicing. The woman who can play a piano concerto, was not able to perform the first time she sat down at a piano. It would have taken years of practice to find the ability to play this level of music. To develop these skills takes dedicated, ongoing effort. This is the way of the recovery life and the way of relationship with God. Practicing these principles in all our affairs is a lifelong process. If we will help others, God will help us. He will use others to bring our lives into balance and the fullness of His joy.

When you think of a helping others ask yourself the following questions:

1. Have you seen someone in need and choose not to offer help?

    _____Yes _____No If yes, describe when and why?

    _____

    _____

2. Who do I routinely see, that has a need I could assist them with? _____

    What is the need? _____

3. What are two life lessons that you have learned that you could use to help others?

    a. _____

    b. _____

4. Have I put the principle of helping others into action in my life?

    _____Yes _____No Give an example:

    _____

    _____

5. Is there anyone that gives me direction in my sobriety? _____Yes _____No

    Who and in what capacity?

    _____

    _____

6. Have I been asked to help out in a service or volunteer job? _____Yes _____No

    What was the job?

    _____

    _____

7. Am I open to perform any task involving helping others, regardless how small or large the task, when I have the ability to do so? _____Yes _____No

8. How has the change in my spiritual life most affected my service to others?

    _____

    _____

9. Describe two things necessary to maintain a life free from addiction?

    1._____

    2. _____

Describe a relationship that represents each of the levels of relationships given. How has it impacted your recovery?

(*Note: An explanation of each is given below.*)

1. Intense:

    _____

    _____

2. Intimate:

    _____

    _____

3. Active:

_____

_____

4. Passive:

_____

_____

5. Casual:

_____

_____

6. Distant:

_____

_____

Levels of Relationship

1. Intense:

Just starting off in the relationship.

Talking daily on phone or seeing frequently at meetings.

Establishing a set of expectations.

What do you want from the relationship and what are the boundaries.

Share problems, challenges, victories.

2. Intimate:

Have become like a family member.

Actively involved in decision making processes.

May communicate several times a day.

Plan around one another.

Describes a more permanent kind of relationship; like you would experience during a tragedy.

Close personal friend.

3. Active:

See and talk to several times a month.

Know about the goings on in one another's lives.

Share problems, challenges, victories.

Consider a personal friend.

4. Passive:

Not currently involved more than occasionally.

May only communicate occasionally, by phone or in passing.

Have been involved in more than one area of their life.

Consider them to be a friend and or sponsor.

5. Casual:

Know a little about the person or their life.

Both maybe in the same home group.

Could be a business or personal relationship.

Talk about getting together for program talk.

6. Distant:

Normally involved in the same groups or meetings.

Focus in when they talk and identify with them.

Met one time.

Recognize on sight.

May or may not know name.

BELIEVE SERVICE TO OTHERS PRIMARILY is about sponsorship and entering into a relationship where you commit to another person to help him or her individually. The real deal is when you have made a commitment to another human being in a one-to-one relationship. It doesn't matter if you are playing the role of the sponsor or the sponsee; in both cases you are helping another in recovery.

David Sutton

Made in the USA
Lexington, KY
28 September 2019